lonely planet

more

ABSURD & AMUSING SIGNS FROM AROUND THE WORLD

SIGNSPOTTING 2

Oncoming vehicles in middle of road

P9-CDA-918

Compiled by Doug Lansky

INTRODUCTION

Perhaps the only thing more staggering than the number of delightfully twisted English signs popping up each year is the spread of English itself. At the moment, roughly two-thirds of the people on the planet speak it as a first, second, or third language, and there are currently seventy-three nations (if you include commonwealths and crown dependencies) where English is officially used. It may not be much of a surprise that India has the world's largest English-speaking population with 350 million, but few would guess that the Philippines has more than twice as many English speakers as Australia; or that China has at least four times as many English speakers as the United Kingdom; or that New Zealand, one of the more famous English-speaking nations, has only the world's twenty-ninth-largest English-speaking population – even Denmark has more citizens who can converse in English.

Just as fascinating is the array of diversity within the English language. Wikipedia now lists 133 regional varieties of English (including twenty-eight just in the United Kingdom). There are also twelve types of official English pidgins and creoles, such as Krio in Sierra Leone, Singlish in Singapore, and Bislama in Vanuatu. Plus there are twenty-seven noted portmanteaus, or newfangled English blends, such as Franglais (French and English) or Chinglish (Chinese and English), or the rather amusingly dubbed Dunglish (Dutch and English). Indeed, the lingual landscape is changing before our eyes.

This may help explain the proliferation of funny signs, at least in part, but it doesn't address the sensitivity. Who are we, after all, to laugh at someone else's mistakes? I think it's a matter of a little self-deprecation. As long as we understand that we'd fare no better trying to put up signs in foreign languages, there's no harm in enjoying the humor of these inadvertent gaffes. Most would readily agree that we Anglophones would have foreign tourists hospitalized with laughter if we tried to be as courteous, sign-wise, to them as they are with us.

There is one strange phenomenon in this regard: many of the very same Anglophones who would eschew responsibility for drafting public messages in a foreign language seem to have no problem offering up their body to other linguistically challenged Anglos with tattoo machines. That is, if neither the tattoo artist nor you speaks, say, Chinese, it would logically follow that there's a reasonable chance a mistake could be made that neither of you would catch. And just a slight deviation in one of those complex symbols might alter the meaning altogether. It may take a trip to China (or the nearest Chinatown) to reveal that the "Inner Strength" shoulder tattoo you picked up in Miami, Dublin, or Auckland is actually proclaiming a weak bladder or a crooked nose. Given the number of such stylized foreign tattoos you see on the beach, at the gym, and on your favorite athletes and actors, it seems statistically likely that a few people (perhaps a thousand) are unwittingly walking around with inked blunders.

I'm no stranger to linguistic gaffes myself. As an expat trying to get by without my mother tongue, I commit more crimes of syntax and mix more metaphors each week than you'll find in the following pages. My six-year-old daughter happily points out most of them, typically in front of visiting guests.

THE AUTHOR

Doug Lansky spent ten years traveling the planet, during which time he visited 120 countries (if you count San Marino). He has written a syndicated newspaper travel column, penned several books, hosted a Discovery Channel show, and delivered his funny presentation on travel around the world. He has moved his base camp numerous times, and is now living in Sweden where he has "the ultimate Ikea kit": a Swedish wife and three daughters. Doug started collecting funny signs during the first year of his travels, and it has turned into a disturbingly addictive habit.

www.signspotting.com

Lions, please turn right. All other big game, straight ahead.

Would hate to see what they charge for overdue library books.

What happens when they let MC Escher design the driver's exam.

LOCATION: LANGLEY, VIRGINIA, USA   CREDIT: STORM CUNNINGHAM

Collect the entire set, including: "The Osama bin Laden Center for Air Safety" and "Bill Clinton Center for Strategic Chastity."

Yo, check out myass.

부드러운 게 튀김

Fried soft Crap

The fried crab is also nice.

Culver's ®

FROZEN CUSTARD
BUTTERBURGERS™

Try Today's Flavor

CARAMEL PECAN
WALLEYE IS BACK

Not sure which sounds less appetizing: the caramel pecan fish or a frozen burger made of butter.

Four-wheel drive and Zoloft are advised.

The 255,026-square-kilometer state will hopefully reopen after renovations.

Presumably it's a buying crossover with the vineyard across the parking lot – a case of Merlot goes great with bags of sheep manure.

Signspotter #37 Karla Richards (hometown: Florence, Italy)

We only went to Ireland because we found one of those super-cheap flights from Pisa to Dublin – it was free, so we only had to pay for airport taxes. My husband, Guido, and I stayed just five days.

We normally eschew tours, but we heard the Irish countryside was spectacular and didn't feel like renting a car. The other tourists on the minibus were fun, mostly aged twenty-five to thirty-five, but the guide was sixty-five and he was spitting out trite memorized comments for the duration of the tour. Not the most exciting day of my travels. We were taken to see a place where they harvest peat moss.

One of the funniest moments was our pit stop for a "a real Irish tea and snack included with the tour." For this, the guide pulled the minibus over to the side of the road, took out a thermos and poured us all a cup of tea in a plastic cup and gave us each a cookie. Not quite what we had envisioned.

At one stop, I saw the sign in the distance and thought it must be wrong. I went to have a closer look and half of the tour group followed. We all had a bit of a chuckle. The German couple posed next to the sign.

If it had been summer, we might have tried walking on the water, but it was a cold, damp October day, so we gave it a miss.

Messiah Crossing?

15

Sadly, the irony is lost on the bears.

LOCATION: SAN CARLOS, CALIFORNIA, USA   CREDIT: LEO DUERR

Clearly someone found their true calling.

LOCATION: GOLD BEACH, OREGON, USA CREDIT: MARK BUTTERFIELD

Let's put a stop to curry once and for all.

ประเจิ๊บน

MILK CHOCOLATE COVERED

CROCODILE

黑褐乳色鳄鱼

LOCATION: BANGKOK, THAILAND   CREDIT: RENATA RHODES

Hold the whipped cream.

LOCATION: SCOTLAND   CREDIT: BRENDA GOTTLIEB

Wanted: marketing director to help town jumpstart tourism.

Filth cleaned here.

Say it five times fast.

Only authorized unauthorized visits.

Nothing quite says "I love my country" like dropping off some hazardous waste.

You know tourists, always smacking their heads into everything. Finally, a helpful reminder.

LOCATION: FLUSHING, NEW YORK, USA CREDIT: YOUNG WHAN CHOI

Wow, your sparkling white armpits look fantastic!

Please do not Annoy, Torment, Pester, Molest, Worry, Badger Harry, Harass, Hackle, Persecute, Irk, Rag, Vex, Bother, Tease, Nettle, Tantalise or Ruffle the Anima

भंडावू , अस्वस्थ, झुलवू , निराश, हाल, व्याकूळ करू नका दुःख, त्रास, इजा
डिवचू , छळू , मारू, हेळसांड, चिडवू नका. क्षुब्ध करू नका.
ोंगाट, आवाज टाळा. हुसकू नका. हल्ला करू नका. मारू नका. उपद्रव देऊ नव
सताऊ नका यातना वेदना देऊ नका. पिडा, छेडू , खोड्या काढू नका.

Microsoft Word synonym generator seems to be working.

LOCATION: GOSPORT, HAMPSHIRE, ENGLAND   CREDIT: ASHLEY TOOZE

Ever wondered where suicide bombers go for a holiday?

公众场所，
贵重物品妥善保管！
Please take care of your values!

Philosophical crimes ahead.

Scool speling knot committed to highist standard.

LAKEVIEW
FUNERAL HOME

an official member of
XL CORPORATION

BU FF ET AND DINNER
CARRY OUT
D ELIVERY
3 54 9006

Presumably, kidney and liver dishes are not on the menu.

터키 전통
산양유
아이스크림

Turkey
Icecream
with
Goat's Milk

トルコの
伝統的な
アイスクリーム

Move over Häagen-Dazs!

LOCATION: LAC DU FLAMBEAU, WISCONSIN, USA   CREDIT: BARBARA FISHER

Yummy!

BEWARE OF BABOONS & MONKEYS!!
- KEEP ALL FOOD STUFF LOCKED AWAY
- CLOSE THE POP–UP ROOF OF THE CARAVAN
- REPORT ANY BABOON ACTIVITY IN THE CAMP TO THE BABOON HOTLINE (082 802 1201)

HAVE A PLEASANT STAY

LOCATION: KRUGER NATIONAL PARK, SOUTH AFRICA   CREDIT: SHERRY YAMAMOTO

Good morning, baboon hotline, how can I help you today?

Signspotter #211 Roberta Rubenstein (hometown: Santa Barbara, California, USA)

I snapped this picture in the center of London, near Leicester Square on Charing Cross Road, waiting for a signal light to change so that I could cross the heavily trafficked street. I actually saw the sign a day earlier but didn't have my camera with me.

My husband and I nearly doubled over with laughter when we saw it, yet tried not to become two of the pedestrian casualties hinted at in the sign.

Just before I took the photo I was wandering around London – a repeat visit to one of my favorite places. I lived in the city for several years at an earlier time in my life and have since returned a number of times.

I think the bystanders did regard me rather strangely as I tried to get into the best position for taking a close-up of the sign, but I was too intent on my photo op to pay much attention. As I recall, I had to wait a while for traffic and pedestrians to pass so that there were no obstructions.

The best sign that "got away" was one advertising the office of a Maine psychiatrist, Dr Les Moody. I was camera-free at the time.

Next of kin will be notified of the experiment results.

LOCATION: PUEBLO, COLORADO, USA   CREDIT: EMILY HARGRAVES

If you can get enough speed on the off ramp, you might just make it.

Come for the food, stay for the waiting.

LOCATION: PUERTO VALLARTA, MEXICO   CREDIT: ERIC PIVNIK

Exclusive club open to all.

LOCATION: RICHFIELD, WISCONSIN, USA   CREDIT: KEITH KOPPEN

You're not going to believe this, but see that big hill in front of you?
Well, it's blocking the view of what's on the other side. No, seriously. It is.

LOCATION: GOLDEN GATE BRIDGE, SAN FRANCISCO, CALIFORNIA, USA
CREDIT: CRISTEN RENE ANDREWS

You're on your own. Good luck!

LOCATION: KATHMANDU, NEPAL   CREDIT: SEAN RANNEY

Old-school brain surgery.

Finally, some alcoholic beverages that the kids can enjoy too.

In Chinese, it makes perfect sense.

Scientists are thrilled with the results since moving on from spleen-based learning.

Translation provided by 50 Cent.

VIEW
ROUGH BUTT BALD
ELEV. 5925
ELEV. HERE 5300

This is apparently what happens when you let seven-year-olds vote on the name.

CHECK YOUR
DEPTH
BEFORE
ENTERING

LOCATION: OPIKI, NEW ZEALAND   CREDIT: RALPH SAMUELSON

Deep thinkers ahead.

注意安全!
TAKE CARE!

小心落水!
FALL INTO WATER CAREFULLY!

Uncontrolled falling will be penalized.

LOCATION: APACHE JUNCTION, ARIZONA, USA   CREDIT: MIKE BROWN

Further up, it turns into Hilarious Valley Trail.

ANYONE. CAUGHT. SHOPLIFTER WILL
BE SHOT 100 TIMES THE VALUE OF THE
STOLEN ITEM (S)

ขโมยสินค้าปรับ 100 เท่า

In other words, steal some chewing gum and your body gets more holes than a sponge.
Amazing that there's a single Thai word for all that.

LOCATION: NEAR MAMMOTH CAVE, KENTUCKY, USA · CREDIT: JIM LEAVER

Let the good times roll at Golgotha.

"சிறுநீர் கழிக்காதீர்
மீறினால் தண்டிக்கப்படுவீர்"

DON'T PASS URINE

VIOLATOO WOULD BE PUNISHED

மேலாளர்
தேவசம் போர்டு கன்னியாகுமரி.

செயல் அலுவலர்
கன்னியாகுமரி பேரூராட்சி

Sounds like some sort of twisted game of traveler Monopoly.
Do not pass urine, do not collect $200.

Signspotter #117 Ken Stern (hometown: Brooklyn, New York, USA)

I took this photo early morning in Agra, India, next to an outdoor street food stall in the middle of town. It was a brisk sunny day. I was just beginning a three-week independent tour of Rajasthan with my wife, Deborah Jacobs, and Jack, our eight-year-old son. My brother-in-law was joining us for a few days. We had just seen the Taj Mahal – a lifelong dream – the day before.

When I saw this sign I wondered if the English school proprietor, Anu Sharma, knew what he had wrought. As an international branding and marketing research consultant myself, I want to believe the naming and graphic treatment was a component of a brilliantly conceived and executed marketing strategy.

To be fair, my brother-in-law pointed to it first. I automatically reached for my camera.

When traveling, we always go native as far as food goes. Needless to say, we partake at every opportunity. When we came upon this sign, we were waiting for our morning breakfast of lassi (yogurt drink) and puffy puri bread with a green-curry-based dipping sauce at a food stall.

I love taking pictures of unusual signs. Hands down this is my favorite.

You'll be speaking like an anus in no time.

53

The foot was last seen with a blister and matching set of bunions. It is armed and fungal.

Either an odd way to prevent tourists from boarding or it's the transport for a losing team's road trip.

No, we're not just waiving the joining fee, we're giving it away! For free!

Talk about overprotective parents. Next I suppose they'll want to move the target range away from the daycare center.

Unrealistic expectations?

How, exactly, are you supposed to adjust your driving for this?

LOCATION: IDAHO, USA
CREDIT: KAY KINDIG

LOCATION: BEDLAM, ENGLAND
CREDIT: ELEANORE MILLER

LOCATION: PORTISHEAD, ENGLAND
CREDIT: JOHN MAKINSON

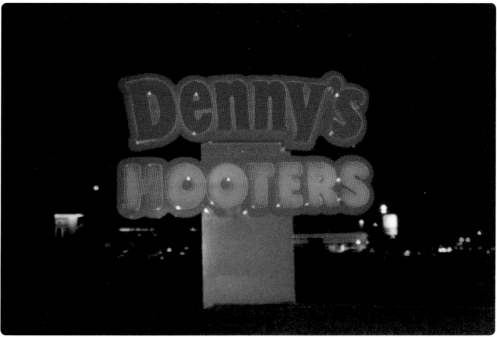

Fast-food merger or gynecomastia?

If you drive past this point, your car may suddenly burst into flames.

Here's an odd mix of sensibilities: thoughtful enough to put up the sign, cruel enough to put the restroom up a flight of stairs.

Pssst, don't tell anyone.

LOCATION: DARWIN, AUSTRALIA   CREDIT: ANDREW BALK

LOCATION: KWAZULU NATAL, SOUTH AFRICA   CREDIT: CASSANDRA ADAMS

Finally, a Carmen Miranda free zone.

I believe our fingers have already met.

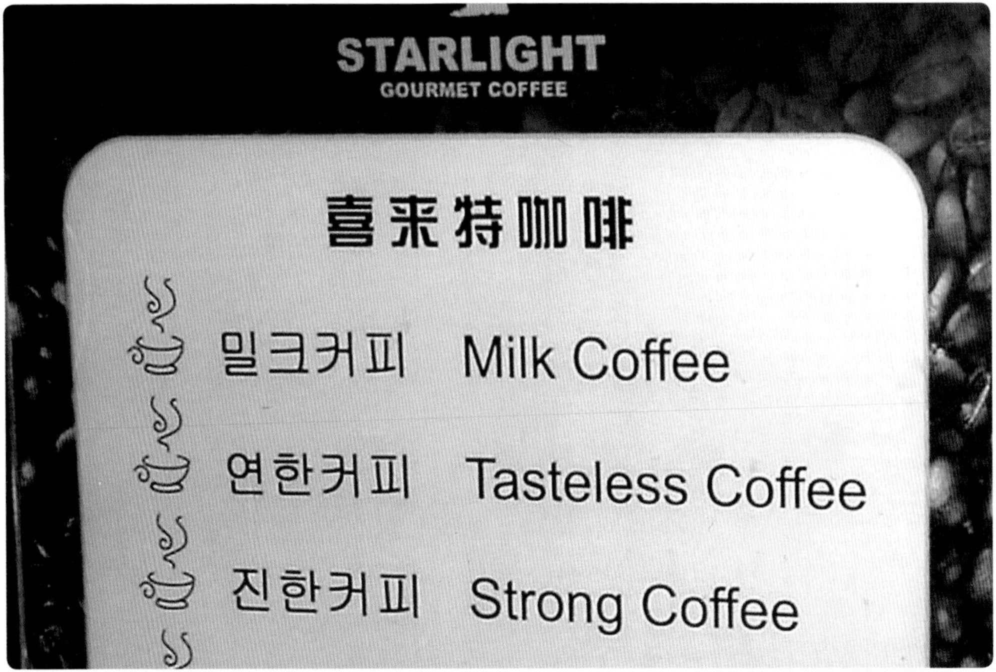

STARLIGHT
GOURMET COFFEE
喜来特咖啡
밀크커피 Milk Coffee
연한커피 Tasteless Coffee
진한커피 Strong Coffee

LOCATION: BEIJING, CHINA CREDIT: STERLING BELL

Now with less taste than ever.

Sad ending to a good street.

There was a time back in primary school when most of us would have gladly paid $5.99 to not get a wedgie.

Under normal conditions, of course, all aircraft would come to a complete stop when passing over a stop sign.

World's smallest demilitarized zone. Please step under this tiny roof if you wish to stay alive.

危　険 ■ 熱湯に注意
柵の中に入らないで下さい。

DANGER ■ If you fall in the pond
you will be boiled

...and then tarred and feathered.

LOCATION: NEENAH, WISCONSIN, USA   CREDIT: SUE BAYER-JABB

This is what happens when fortune-cookie writers are forced to seek employment elsewhere.

LOCATION: BETWEEN LAS VEGAS AND LOS ANGELES, USA   CREDIT: MARK PERMAN

Little pronunciation tip: the second "z" is silent.

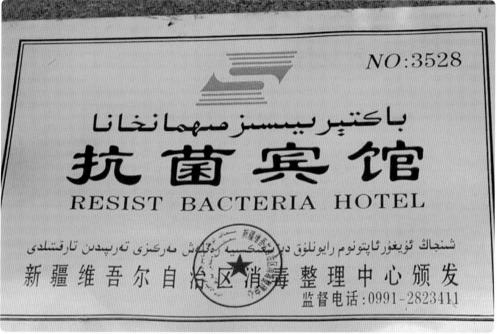

NO:3528

باكتېرىيسىز مېهمانخانا

抗菌宾馆

RESIST BACTERIA HOTEL

شىنجاڭ ئۇيغۇر ئاپتونوم رايونلۇق دېزىنفېكسىيە كەڭەش مەركىزى تەرىپىدىن تارقىتىلدى

新疆维吾尔自治区消毒整理中心颁发

监督电话:0991-2823411

LOCATION: KASHGAR, CHINA CREDIT: JENNNY ANDERSEN

This one received some sort of star – possibly for excellence in antiseptics.

Police are cracking down on either swearing or flagrant punctuation abuse.

Party of one, right this way please.

Dying for a bargain.

Just a suggestion.

LOCATION: ATACAMA, CHILE   CREDIT: HUGO COELHO

Signspotter #343 Alexandra Watkins (hometown: San Francisco, California, USA)

This was a stop on my six-month trip down the east coast of Australia. I started in Cape Tribulation and worked my way down to Sydney. I had about a week in Port Townsend.

When I first saw the sign it reminded me of that Michael Moore film *Pets or Meat,* where a woman has rabbits available for people to buy and keep as pets or slaughter for the meat. I figured this store was where they killed the pets and sold them as meat.

OK, that's not what it turned out to be but I still thought the aisles of refrigerated pet food were a total culture shock. Some of it was actually fresh kangaroo meat. They're feeding cute little kangaroos to their dogs and cats! And the butcher told me that people may buy better cuts of meat for their pets than they do for themselves.

I thought pet owners in San Francisco spoiled their pets, but they've got nothing on Australians.

What'll it be, filet meow or hot dog?

请勿乱扔杂物

PLEASE DON'T THROW RUBBISH AWAY

ごみを捨てないでください

Forbidden City forbids trash.

LOCATION: POCATELLO, IDAHO, USA   CREDIT: MAUREEN WITWER

Discreet snickering OK.

LOCATION: KANSASVILLE, WISCONSIN, USA   CREDIT: ANDREA UGENT

Dude, where's my car?

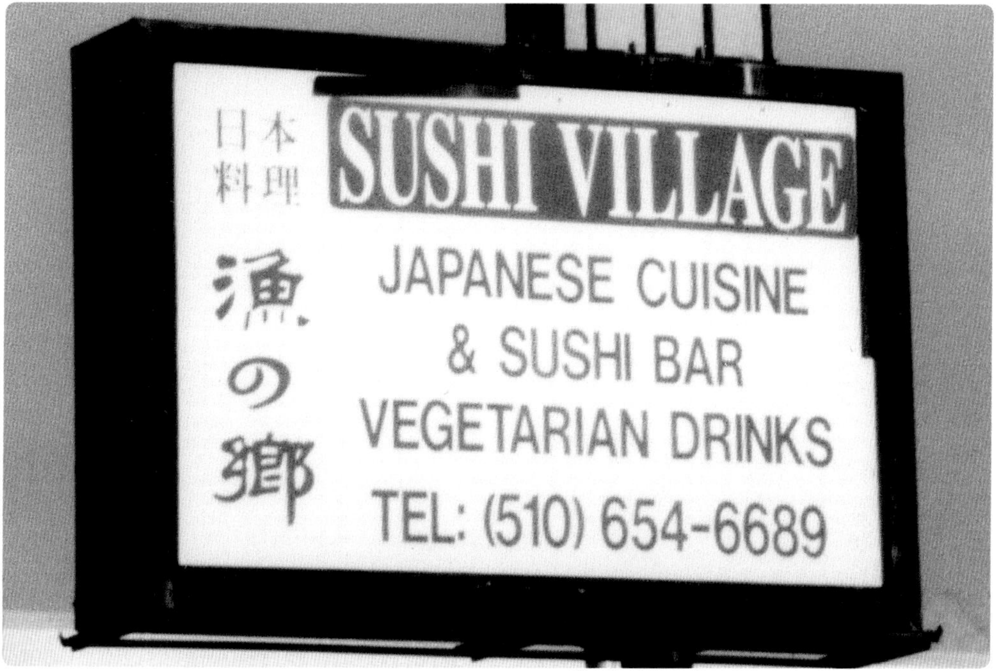
日本料理
SUSHI VILLAGE
漁の郷
JAPANESE CUISINE
& SUSHI BAR
VEGETARIAN DRINKS
TEL: (510) 654-6689

LOCATION: EMERYVILLE, CALIFORNIA, USA CREDIT: ALPHONSO JACKSON

Introducing meat-free beverages.

ODUM'S
BARBER SHOP
TANNING BED
WE REPAIR 8.00
HAIRCUTS FOR10

95-19

LOCATION: FLAGLER BEACH, FLORIDA, USA   CREDIT: BRENDA WINKELMAN

So, first they give you an $8 haircut, then they repair it for $10?
Still a better deal than one of those overpriced $20 haircuts.

82

Welcome to Miami, now conveniently located inside to help combat the stifling summer humidity.
Seniors will particularly appreciate the ground-floor access.

LOCATION: POINT REYES STATION, CALIFORNIA, USA   CREDIT: AME GALLOWAY

Hard to imagine how this one plays out: "OK, that'll be one number two and two number ones. Please pull up to the window."

Should I stay or should I go now?

If the adjacent cemetery is any indication, this sign doesn't seem to be very effective. Maybe a crossing guard would help. Or, from the looks of the sign, a chiropractor.

They're basically saying, "Our products could cost virtually any ridiculous, hyper-inflated amount, possibly into the millions, but never less than $10!" Apparently, it's a stroke of marketing genius, as there are offices in London and Paris as well.

LOCATION: BATALHA, PORTUGAL   CREDIT: PAUL PHILLIPS

Well, at least you know where it is now.

All other body parts OK to wash.

Mmmm...haven't had a taste of that for a while.

Possible slogan: we keep working until you've got hazyview!

"Alternative fuel" or even "natural gas" might be more appropriate.

PHẠT PHÚC NOODLE BAR

PHẠT PHÚC
NOODLE BAR

Authentic Vietnamese
Noodle Soup

Hard to believe, but in Vietnamese, the name actually translates as "Happy Buddha."

With supporters like you…

How convenient to get those sexually transmitted diseases treated just a few steps from the confessional.

Signspotter #95 David Anderson (hometown: White Salmon, Washington, USA)

We saw this sign on our way to or from Kildrummy Castle. After taking the photo, we decided to follow the sign and see where it would take us. We weren't lost before we saw the sign, but we had no idea where we were once we started following that road. It was about five or ten kilometers before we reached Lost, a community of artisans.

This was a castle-themed trip. We saw about fifty castles around Scotland in two and a half weeks. My wife was pregnant with our first child and we wanted to squeeze in one last independent trip.

Unfortunately, at the first whisky stop or two, just the smell made my wife queasy (she was in her second trimester). For me, it wasn't easy driving by all those great single-malt distilleries.

The most baffling thing about signs is that, in Scotland, there seems to be one for the smallest of towns – even ones with a single building. So it was common that we'd follow a sign and not know when we actually reached the place or if we had blinked and passed it.

So it really is possible to get lost and know exactly where you are.

CLOTHES MUST BE
REMOVED
WHEN FINISHED

CLOTHES MAY BE
REMOVED BY
WAITING CUSTOMERS
OR MANAGEMENT

LOCATION: ALAMEDA, CALIFORNIA, USA   CREDIT: NICOLE CLAUSING

I'll hold him down, you grab his socks.

If only they'd enforce this in doctors' offices.

Think your date is going to get suspicious if you take her here?

Table Mountain National Park

Warning
Please look under your vehicles for penguins

Sponsored by
Boulders
Beach
Lodge

The diagram in the lower left looks more like the penguins are simply providing a free brake inspection, or maybe changing the oil.

Don't worry, it's only gunfire.

Brace for head-on collison.

Better fasten your seatbelt.

You can almost imagine the local newspaper headline: "Player shot while shooting."

LOCATION: NORTHERN IRELAND
CREDIT: BILL SELF

LOCATION: WELLINGTON, NEW ZEALAND
CREDIT: RALPH SAMUELSON

LOCATION: GRAFTON, WISCONSIN, USA
CREDIT: JAMES BUCHHOLZ

WARNING!

DO NOT RAM GATE.

CAR DAMAGE WILL RESULT!

ONE CAR ONLY

Hey, let's go ram that large metal gate. No, wait. Check that out. It's going to damage the car.

LOCATION: TAICHUNG, TAIWAN   CREDIT: JAMIE RASKIN

Honey, I don't care if it's 3am, I need a radish right now.

Signspotter #392 Josh Kaplan (hometown: San Francisco, California, USA)

I was traveling around the world with Jenny, my girlfriend. We were on the road from Arusha to the Ngorongoro Crater, about to camp out with the wildebeests in the crater highlands.

We made our driver reverse the car to see if the sign actually said what we thought it said, and then I snapped the photo.

The road was under construction, and the sign was before an uphill bend. I believe they meant "You can't see who might be coming down around this bend." Certainly a creative way to phrase it.

The funniest part was when I got out to take the photo, I was asked by the local Tanzanian workers if I was Japanese (I look about as white American as you get). It turned out the contract for the road was being funded by a Japanese organization, and he assumed I was working for them — why else would I photograph a construction sign?

You never know when invisibility is going to strike.

TATTOOS
FOR LEASE
STARTING AT $7.00 SQ.FT.

Interesting business idea. Getting them back might be a bit tricky.

Why not just call it "Five-Star-Ultra-Chic-Spa-Hotel-and-Golf-Club-Rated-Number-One-by-*Condé Nast Traveller*" Hotel?

107

A cut above the rest.

LOCATION: LONDON, ENGLAND   CREDIT: APRIL ORCUTT

It's not high-tech or low-tech, but somewhere in between. Perhaps something like the instruction manual for an iPod.

How the local police department plans to finance their next party.

We double dare you.

Hey Mom, guess what? I'm living the dream.

Proudly encouraging eco-terrorism since 2001.

You can walk in any time you like, but you can never leave.

Please help confine nudity to the bushes and the face of the mountain.

Business is booming.

Signspotter #246 Rosie Barber (hometown: Hudson, Wisconsin, USA)

On this trip my husband, Ed, and I went to see the Bay of Fundy – 2000 kilometers each way (we drove). It's got the highest tide in the world. Strange to be walking on the seabed and know that in a few hours the water will be about fifteen meters deep in that spot.

I remember the sign was on the left-hand side of a country road. Ed was driving. I said, we should probably take a photo of that sign, so we turned the car around.

The sign was strange, but we also looked around the cemetery. There's only about twenty-five people buried there, but the tombstones are strange, sort of shaped like the upper half of a person's body, skinny and tall with shoulders and a head. It's an old cemetery, not so well kept.

We also stopped at Acadia National Park in Maine. You can drive to the top of Cadillac Mountain and there's a sign stating that's where the sun's rays first hit US soil in the morning.

We are senior citizen vagabonds, retired with a small RV. We recently drove to Alaska and Mexico as well.

Ha ha! You're dead! Evidently someone else had the last laugh.

LOCATION: FISH HOEK, SOUTH AFRICA   CREDIT: GARRET IPPOLITO

Perhaps not the best PR for the police when they need private security to protect their own station.

She did what?

We've the best selection of dead horses you'll ever see. Great for beginners.

LOCATION: NORWAY   CREDIT: DOUG LANSKY

Too much yeast?

Wasn't the whole point of valet parking to keep your car from being at risk?

衝突注意

Clash

LOCATION: TOKYO, JAPAN   CREDIT: MICHELLE SIMON

Introducing… The Clash.

غرفـة العبـاءات
للعرب والأجانب

PUTTING.ON SPECIAL
CLOTHES ROOM

←

For that special look.

BEACH RULES
1. NO RUNNING ON DOCK
2. NO PUSHING, SHOVING or DUNKING
3. NO THROWING STONES, SAND or MUD
4. NO MALICIOUS CANNONBALLING
5. NO SWIMMING BEYOND OUTER ROPES
6. NO SWIMMING UNDER DOCK
7. NO MORE THAN 1 PERSON On Diving Boards at a Time
8. NO HANGING ON BARRELS or ROPES
9. NO OBSCENE LANGUAGE
10. NO JUMPING or DIVING WHERE PROHIBITED
11. NO FLOTATION DEVICES Beyond Inner Ropes
12. NO SWIMMING during SWIMMING LESSONS
13. LIFEGUARDS RESERVE RIGHT to 2 pm BREAK
14. NO ANIMALS ALLOWED ON BEACH
15. NO ALCOHOLIC BEVERAGES ALLOWED on BEACH
NO LITTERING
KEEP YOUR BEACH CLEAN

Welcome to happy fun beach.

Tragic – he didn't even live long enough to check the spelling on his sign.

OK, we get it.

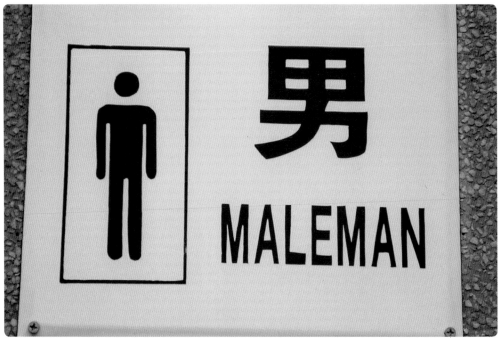

Restroom, mail delivery, or testosterone replacement therapy…you decide.

LOCATION: ELY, NEVADA, USA   CREDIT: RICHARD SILVEIRA

Nice to see Gary Larson is keeping busy.

The road less traveled.

请勿戏弄动物

Please don't hurt the animals while teasing them

Names OK, no sticks and stones.

AL MUMTAZS
BUTT FOODS
(416) 285-5071
لحـم حـلال گوشت

Bottom feeder.

LOCATION: WALLINGTON, NEW JERSEY, USA   CREDIT: FRANK SACCOMANNO

Funeral home drive-thru – for those in a hurry to get back on the road.

Cleverly avoiding the word "fat."

Interesting… Cassowary birds are a better speeding deterrent than police.

We've got more Christians than we know what to do with and they're priced so low we're practically giving them away.

교통불편신고센타
(Intercourse Discomfort Report Center)

777-5000

교통종합민원센타

〈서울 특별 시〉

Press one for chafing, two for itching, or three for general irritation.

Way off piste.

Signspotter #185 Jessica Vapnek (hometown: Rome, Italy)

When I saw this sign at the train station, my friend was already on the train waiting for me. We were heading to Madurai.

We had been traveling for two weeks around Tamil Nadu. My friend's great-aunt Ida Scudder founded the Christian Medical Center one hundred years ago (with one bed) and it's now among the best in India. We were there to celebrate the centennial.

The moment I saw the sign I quickly rummaged around for my camera (as if someone was going to run up and paint over the sign that very instant!).

I didn't expect to feel any guilt, but there's always the chance that when people see you taking a picture of a sign and laughing, they think you're laughing at them.

Besides the sign, I spotted a Bollywood romance being filmed in a botanical garden. On a dare, we approached the main romantic lead and had our pictures taken with him. Unfortunately, the photo never turned out.

AVOID

SLEEPING NEAR THE WINDOWS,
WEARING HEAVY JEWELS, LEAVING
THE LUGGAGES AS ABANDONED,
FRIENDSHIP WITH STRANGERS,
VICTIMS OF SPURIOUS DRINKS,
BE ALERT THROUGHOUT THE JOURNEY.

Have a pleasant journey.

EXIT 10

857

Cheat Lake
Fairchance Rd.

7% GRADE

Someone on the naming commission has got a sense of justice. Or humor.

Who knew safety was such a high-risk activity?

卤煮火烧
Boiledcake

炒疙瘩
Fried pimple

碗

碗

Don't knock it until you've tried it. Might be good.

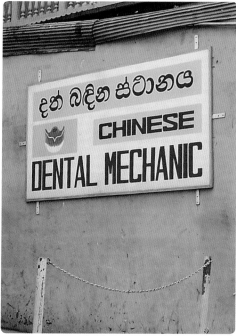

Pimp my teeth.

For some reason, I never imagined that
sidewalks actually ended.

EXIT 192

Bad Route Road
↗

REST AREA

Better get some rest first.

America may be taking the super-size concept a little too far.

Motto: we stay busy to maintain the process of appearing to get things done.

OK, we need a name that's respectable, yet captures the essence of what we do, and makes the Spanish-speaking community feel welcome. Any ideas?

More tourists are coming every year.

When you put it that way, it hardly seems like a mugging.

It's just a matter of fine breeding and proper education.

Yes, baldness is just around the corner.

Without this sign, you'd never know that you need to increase your speed to clear the rocks below.

Hours of fun for the whole family.

LOCATION: KISUMU, KENYA   CREDIT: LAWRENCE WORCESTER

The art of reckless driving.

743 **Greacus Gym** T

ΤΗΡΙΟ-ΠΑΘΗΤΙΚΗ ΓΥΜΝΑΣΤΙΚΗ-ΜΕΘΟΔΟΣ INC

Pathetic Health Studio

Join now and we'll have you looking pathetic in just a few weeks!

Babies and Children

BUY 2 GET 3 FREE!

OPEN

Minivan sold separately.

当心滑跌
DON'T FALL DOWN

Fallen pedestrians will be fined.

此博物馆每日消毒

Our Museum is disinfected
Every day

Sanitized for your protection.

On the bright side, at least it's not a question mark.

LOCATION: ABU DHABI, UNITED ARAB EMIRATES   CREDIT: VANCE STEPHENSON

ACKNOWLEDGEMENTS

This book would have been impossible to assemble without the help of the world's largest army of travel photographers. Nearly 20,000 of you have sent in images since 2000 when this funny-sign project began. As a single human trying to review, catalog, resize, and caption them all (and help raise three kids), it's been difficult to keep everyone updated on the status of their submission. Thank you not just for your photos, but for your patience in this regard.

I'd like to continue by thanking Spud Hilton and Henrik Harr for providing hours of free feedback in return for – get this – a mention on this page. Also thanks to Rachel Williams and Ellie Cobb, my editors at Lonely Planet, Michael Bourret, my agent, and Tony Wheeler for green lighting the first *Signspotting* book back in 2004. Getting *Signspotting 2* from a large Microsoft Word file to a carefully cut slap of dead tree with its own barcode is an enormous team effort, and I'm grateful to the extremely talented, charming, good looking (and modest) design, PR, sales, and marketing people at Lonely Planet who have given this project such a generous amount of their time.

Thanks to Markus Rutiger at the Star Alliance for, thus far, providing a round-the-world ticket each year for the best sign.

Finally, I'd like to thank my wife, who has, each of the 5000 times I've said "Hey, come and check out this one – it's hilarious," actually come over and checked it out.

SIGNSPOTTING 2
More Absurd & Amusing Signs from Around the World
September 2007
ISBN 978 1 74179 182 2

Published by Lonely Planet Publications Pty Ltd
ABN 36 005 607 983
© Doug Lansky 2007
© photographers as indicated 2007

Cover photographs by
Headlights on road at night, Seth Goldfarb, Getty
Car on Road, Creatas, Photolibrary

Printed through The Bookmaker International Ltd.
Printed in Hong Kong

Publisher Roz Hopkins
Senior Commissioning Editor Ellie Cobb
Commissioning Editor Rachel Williams
Design James Hardy
Layout Jim Hsu, Mik Ruff
Editors David Carroll, Sasha Baskett

LONELY PLANET OFFICES
AUSTRALIA
Head Office
Locked Bag 1, Footscray, Victoria 3011
☎ 03 8379 8000, fax 03 8379 8111
talk2us@lonelyplanet.com.au

USA
150 Linden St, Oakland, CA 94607
☎ 510 893 8555, toll free 800 275 8555
fax 510 893 8572, info@lonelyplanet.com

UK
72–82 Rosebery Ave,
Clerkenwell, London EC1R 4RW
☎ 020 7841 9000, fax 020 7841 9001
go@lonelyplanet.co.uk